D1054949

# Arctic Tundra: Land with No Trees

## By Allan Fowler

**Consultants**

Linda Cornwell, Learning Resource Consultant,
Indiana Department of Education

Fay Robinson, Child Development Specialist

Lynne Kepler, Educational Consultant

Children's Press®
A Division of Grolier Publishing
New York   London   Hong Kong   Sydney
Danbury, Connecticut

Project Editor: Downing Publishing Services
Designer: Herman Adler Design Group
Photo Researcher: Caroline Anderson

**Library of Congress Cataloging-in-Publication Data**

Fowler, Allan.
    Arctic tundra: land with no trees / by Allan Fowler.
        p. cm. – (Rookie read-about science)
    Includes index.
    Summary: Describes the climate as well as plant, animal, and
human life in the nearly treeless area spread across northern parts
of Canada, Alaska, Europe, and Asia.
    ISBN 0-516-20032-1 (lib. bdg.) — ISBN 0-516-26079-0 (pbk.)
    1. Tundra ecology—Arctic regions—Juvenile literature.
2. Tundras—Arctic regions—Juvenile literature. [1. Tundra ecology.
2. Tundras. 3. Arctic regions. 4. Ecology.] I. Title. II. Series.
QH541.5.T8F68    1996
575.5'2644–dc20                         96-14005
                                      CIP
                                       AC

12 13 14 15 16 17 18 19 20 R 09 08 07 06

Here is a pleasant summer scene. You see grass and pretty flowers but no trees. You are looking at an arctic tundra.

A tundra is a cold, nearly treeless area.

If you dug a hole in the ground there — a hole about one foot deep — you would reach frozen soil.

All year long, even during the summer, this subsoil remains frozen.

frozen subsoil (permafrost)

A tree needs deep, unfrozen
soil to sink its roots into.

That's why there are no trees
on a tundra, except for a
few tiny, or dwarf, trees.

Tundras are spread across the northern parts of Canada, Alaska, Europe, and Asia.

These lands are close to the North Pole, so they are called arctic tundras.

arctic tundra

Other tundras are at the tops of mountains. They are called alpine tundras.

alpine tundra

Arctic tundras are covered
by snow more than half
the year.

The summers are short —
and the temperature
in summer doesn't get
much higher than about
50 degrees.

No wonder the subsoil
never thaws out!

But arctic tundras are full
of life.  Many kinds of
plants and animals thrive
in a cold climate.

# Reindeer and caribou . . .

caribou

arctic fox

foxes and wolves . . . grizzly
bears and polar bears . . .

arctic hares and rodents
called lemmings . . . are
at home in the tundra.

arctic hare

So is this musk-ox,
which looks like a
small, shaggy bison.

Seals and walruses come
ashore where the tundra
meets the sea.

All these animals have heavy coats to help keep them warm.

The ermine's fur turns white in winter.

Wolves or foxes, hunting for prey, might not see an ermine against the white snow.

ermine

stoat

For summer, the ermine
turns brown — and is
then known as a stoat.

Arctic char is one of the few kinds of fish found in rivers and lakes of tundra regions.

arctic char

Geese, terns, and some other birds of the arctic tundra fly south every fall, and return in the spring to nest.

arctic tern and chick

caribou herd

Herds of reindeer and caribou also move south, or migrate, in the fall. It's easier for them to find food where the climate is warmer.

reindeer moss lichen

After the winter's snow
has finally melted, grasses,
shrubs, moss, and flowers
appear. Reindeer graze
on lichens, plants that
usually grow on rocks.

The tundra is home to very few people. Those who live in the Canadian and Alaskan tundra are sometimes called Eskimos.

But their proper name —
the name they call
themselves — is Inuit.

Their life is hard and food
is scarce.

The Inuit have had to be
very clever to survive.

Inuit whalers hauling their catch to shore

Inuit child ice fishing

They hunt seals, caribou, bears, and other animals for food.

They use the skins of these animals for clothing . . . and to cover the Inuits' kayaks, or canoelike boats.

How would you like to live the life of an Inuit?

# Words You Know

alpine tundra

arctic tundra

caribou

arctic char

ermine

arctic fox

goose

arctic hare

30

Inuits

lemming

lichens

musk-ox

reindeer

terns

seals          walrus

arctic wolf

# Index

## About the Author

Allan Fowler is a free-lance writer with a background in advertising.
Born in New York, he lives in Chicago now and enjoys traveling.

## Photo Credits

Visuals Unlimited — ©Steve McCutcheon, cover, 5, 28; ©J.D. Cunningham, 10,
30 (top left); ©Charles Preitner, 11, 30 (top right); ©Tom J. Ulrich, 17, 31 (bottom
left); ©Jane McAlonan, 31 (bottom right)

Valan Photos — ©John Eastcott/YVA Momatiuk, 3; ©J.R.Page, 6; ©Stephen J.
Krasemann, 7, 9, 13, 20 30 (center left); ©Wayne Lankinen, 14, 30 (bottom left); 19,
30 (center right); ©Albert Kuhnigk, 16, 31 (center left); ©Gilbert Van Ryckevorsel,
21, 30 (center middle); ©Pam E. Hickman, 24, 31 (top right); ©Kennon Cooke, 25,
31 (top left); ©Fred Bruemmer, 27; ©James M. Richards, 30 (bottom middle); ©Hälle
Flygare, 31 (center middle)

Alaska Stock Images — ©Tom Soucek, 15, 30 (bottom right); ©Harry Walker, 22,
31 (center right); ©Johnny Johnson, 23; ©George Herben, 31 (top middle)

COVER: Fireweed in arctic tundra, Northwest Territories, Canada